I DECLARE

INTRODUCTION

Our words have creative power. Whenever we speak something, either good or bad, we give life to what we are saying. Too many people say negative things about themselves, about their families, and about their futures.

They don't realize they are prophesying their futures. The Scripture says, "We will eat the fruit of our words." That means we will get exactly what we've been saying.

Here is the key; you've got to send your words out in the direction you want your life to go. You cannot talk defeat and expect to have victory. You can't talk deficiency and expect to have abundance. You will produce what you say. If you want to know what you will be like five years from now, just listen to what you are saying about yourself. With our words we can either bless our futures or we can curse them.

I have written this book of thirty-one declarations so you can bless your future one day at a time, one month at

I DECLARE

*31 Promises to Speak
Over Your Life*

JOEL OSTEEN

Running Press
Philadelphia • LONDON

A Running Press® Miniature Edition™
© 2014 by Joel Osteen

Printed in China

9 8 7 6 5 4 3 2 1
Digit on the right indicates the number of this printing

Library of Congress Control Number: 2014934453

ISBN 978-0-7624-5487-7

Running Press Book Publishers
A Member of the Perseus Books Group
2300 Chestnut Street
Philadelphia, PA 19103-4371

Visit us on the web!
www.runningpress.com

a time. My hope is that you will take just a moment each day to bless your future with one of these positive, inspiring, and encouraging declarations. If you read one declaration and story each day, I believe you will put yourself in a position for God's blessings.

Use this book as your guide for declaring your victory each day. Declare health. Declare favor. Declare abundance.

Have a report of victory.

You are one of a kind. You are a masterpiece. You are a prized possession. When you wake up in the morning and look in the mirror instead of getting depressed, you need to smile and say, "Good morning, you beautiful thing. Good morning, you handsome thing. Good morning, you blessed, prosperous, successful, strong, talented, creative, confident, secure, disciplined, focused, highly favored child of the Most High God." Get it on the inside. Speak faith over your future.

DAY ONE

I DECLARE GOD'S INCREDIBLE
BLESSINGS OVER MY LIFE. I WILL SEE
AN EXPLOSION OF GOD'S GOODNESS,
A SUDDEN WIDESPREAD INCREASE.
I WILL EXPERIENCE THE SURPASSING
GREATNESS OF GOD'S FAVOR. IT WILL
ELEVATE ME TO A LEVEL HIGHER
THAN I EVER DREAMED OF.
EXPLOSIVE BLESSINGS
ARE COMING MY WAY.

This is my declaration.

You may think your situation is permanent. You've been in it a long time. You don't see how you could ever rise any higher. All the facts are telling you it's impossible. But God is saying, "You need to get ready. Where you are is not permanent. I have explosive blessings coming your way. I will increase you beyond your salary. I will bless you beyond your normal income. I will suddenly change things in your life."

That's how the word *explosion* is defined. It means a "sudden, widespread increase." That's what God wants to do for each one of us. Suddenly. You won't expect it. It's out of the ordinary and it's not small. It's not mediocre. It's widespread increase. That means it's so amazing you know it had to be the hand of God.

I'm believing for explosive blessings.

In the real world, it may look like you could never accomplish your dreams. You've already calculated how you'll never get out of debt. You've run all the numbers—but God is saying, "You haven't seen My explosive blessings. You haven't seen the surpassing greatness of My favor. I have blessings that will catapult you years ahead. I have increase that goes beyond your normal calculations."

I've learned God doesn't always take us in normal increments. There are times He will increase us little by little. We have to be faithful day in and day out. But when you come to one of these *explosive* blessings, instead of going from 7 to 8 to 9, God will take you from 7 to 8 to 63 to 64. That's widespread increase!

Day Two

I DECLARE I WILL EXPERIENCE
GOD'S FAITHFULNESS. I WILL NOT
WORRY. I WILL NOT DOUBT. I WILL
KEEP MY TRUST IN HIM, KNOWING
THAT HE WILL NOT FAIL ME. I WILL
GIVE BIRTH TO EVERY PROMISE GOD
PUT IN MY HEART AND I WILL BE-
COME EVERYTHING GOD
CREATED ME TO BE.

This is my declaration.

Every one of us has dreams and goals in our heart. There are promises that we are standing on. Maybe you are believing for a child to turn around, or believing to get healthy again, believing to start a business or to be in ministry. Deep down, you know God has spoken that to your spirit. He has birthed it on the inside. But so often, because it's taking a long time and we've been through disappointments, we get negative and start thinking that it will not happen.

*Just because
you don't see anything
happening doesn't
mean God is not
working.*

God is faithful to His word. All
of His promises are "Yes" and "Amen."
That means if you will do your part
and believe, even though it looks impossible, and not let your mind, your
emotions, or other people talk you out
of it, then God promises in due season
and at the right time, He will bring it

to pass. It may not happen the way you expect it or on your timetable, but God is a faithful God. It will happen.

If we will keep our trust in Him, He will always make a way even though it looks like there is no way. He will give you strength for every battle, wisdom for every decision, peace that passes understanding. God will vindicate you for the wrongs that have been done. He will pay you back for unfair situations. He promised He will not only bring your dreams to pass, but He will give you even the secret desires of your heart.

Dare to trust Him. Come back to that place of peace. Quit being worried, stressed out, wondering if it will happen. God has you in the palm of His hand. He has never once failed before, and the good news is He is not about to start now.

Day Three

I DECLARE I HAVE THE GRACE
I NEED FOR TODAY. I AM FULL OF
POWER, STRENGTH, AND DETERMI-
NATION. NOTHING I FACE WILL BE
TOO MUCH FOR ME. I WILL OVER-
COME EVERY OBSTACLE, OUTLAST
EVERY CHALLENGE, AND COME
THROUGH EVERY DIFFICULTY
BETTER OFF THAN I WAS BEFORE.

This is my declaration.

When the people of Israel were in the wilderness headed toward the Promised Land, God gave them manna each morning to eat. It would appear on the ground. But He specifically instructed them to gather up only enough for one day's supply. In fact, if they took more it wouldn't last. It would spoil. In the same way, God doesn't give us grace for a year at a time, a month at a time.

Every twenty-four hours God has a fresh

new supply of grace,
of favor, of wisdom,
of forgiveness.

How will you make it through the slow season at work? One day at a time.

How will you raise a difficult child? One day at a time.

I heard Corrie ten Boom say something very interesting on this topic. During World War II, she and her Dutch family hid Jews from the Nazis and saved many lives. Eventually, she was caught and put in prison. In the concentration camps, she saw all kinds of atrocities. Through a series of unusual events, Corrie was accidentally released and her life was spared. In spite of seeing all the senseless killings, she never really became bitter. She even forgave the man who killed her family members.

Somebody asked her how she could make it through those dark days of seeing such terrible acts of hatred and still be loving and kind and forgiving. She told of how when she was a little girl, her father would take her on train rides throughout Europe. He would always purchase the tickets several weeks in advance. But he would never give her the ticket until right before they were boarding. Whenever her father saw the headlights of the train pulling into the station, he would hand his little daughter the ticket and they would step onboard together.

Corrie said, "God doesn't give us the grace we need until we're about to step onboard. But if you were to ever go through something like I went through, I can assure you God's grace will be there to help you make it through the dark valleys and still keep your head held high and your heart filled with love."

Now when you come to a dark valley, a difficult season, a sickness, don't worry about it. Your Heavenly Father will hand you the ticket. He will give you the grace, the strength, the favor, the forgiveness to do what you need to do.

Day Four

I DECLARE IT IS NOT TOO LATE TO ACCOMPLISH EVERYTHING GOD HAS PLACED IN MY HEART. I HAVE NOT MISSED MY WINDOW OF OPPORTUNITY. GOD HAS MOMENTS OF FAVOR IN MY FUTURE. HE IS PREPARING ME RIGHT NOW BECAUSE HE IS ABOUT TO RELEASE A SPECIAL GRACE TO HELP ME ACCOMPLISH THAT DREAM. THIS IS MY TIME. THIS IS MY MOMENT. I RECEIVE IT TODAY!

This is my declaration.

Many times we put off what we know God wants us to do. Maybe down deep, God has been dealing with you about forgiving a wrong, getting back in shape, having a better attitude, spending more time with your family. Or maybe it's a dream or goal that you know you should be pursuing.

It's easy to talk yourself out of your dreams and goals. Too many people settle for mediocrity. But the good news is God never aborts a dream. We may give up on them. We may quit pursuing new opportunities, quit believing to overcome an obstacle. But God still has every intention of bringing to pass every dream, every promise, He put in your heart.

You can still become everything God created you to be.

Now you should rise up in faith and say, "This is my time. This is my moment. I'm not settling where I am. I've let excuses hold me back long enough. But today, I will take steps of faith to pursue new opportunities, to explore new hobbies, to break bad habits, to get rid of wrong mindsets. I know it's not too late to accomplish everything God has placed in my heart."

You have to stay passionate about what God put in your heart. Don't let one disappointment, or even a series of disappointments, convince you to give up and settle where you are. I've learned every setback means you're one step closer to seeing the dream come to pass. You have to come to your closed doors before you'll ever get to your open doors. You may have tried and failed a thousand times. But you never know; number one thousand and one may be the door that swings open wide. Get your fire back.

Day Five

I DECLARE I AM GRATEFUL FOR WHO GOD
IS IN MY LIFE AND FOR WHAT HE'S DONE.
I WILL NOT TAKE FOR GRANTED THE
PEOPLE, THE OPPORTUNITIES, AND THE
FAVOR HE HAS BLESSED ME WITH.
I WILL LOOK AT WHAT IS RIGHT AND NOT
WHAT IS WRONG. I WILL THANK HIM FOR
WHAT I HAVE AND NOT COMPLAIN ABOUT
WHAT I DON'T HAVE. I WILL SEE EACH
DAY AS A GIFT FROM GOD. MY HEART
WILL OVERFLOW WITH PRAISE AND
GRATITUDE FOR ALL OF HIS GOODNESS.

This is my declaration.

I talk to people who have had life-threatening experiences, whether from an illness, an accident, or some other challenge, and without fail they talk about how they have come to appreciate each and every day more than ever before. They don't take a minute for granted. They see every day as a gift from God.

We have to realize that our lives could be gone in a moment. There are no guarantees that we will be here at this time next year. Learn to live each day to the fullest. Don't complain. Don't focus on what's wrong. Be grateful for the opportunity to experience each day.

Things may not be perfect. You may have some aches and pains. You may have some adversity. But in the big scope of things, your life could be a whole lot worse.

You need to live every day like it could be your last.

You may not realize it but we are living in the good old days. I'm convinced twenty or thirty years from now you will look back and say, "Those were some great times. I remember when Lakewood was over in East Houston. I remember when Joel was just a young man. I remember when his brother, Paul, still had some hair!" *These* are the good old days.

I used to play basketball with a young man, a strong athlete, who began having problems with one of his eyes. He went to the doctor and was told that he had a form of cancer that threatened his vision in the eye.

As you can imagine, he was devastated. He could not believe it. Then, he went in for surgery and his doctors found that he didn't have cancer. Instead, they found an unusual fungus, which they were able to remove. His vision was saved. When my friend woke up from the operation and heard the good news he said, "This is the greatest day of my life!"

Because he almost lost his vision, seeing has now taken on a whole new meaning. He appreciates it in a much greater way.

Day Six

I DECLARE A LEGACY OF FAITH OVER MY LIFE. I DECLARE THAT I WILL STORE UP BLESSINGS FOR FUTURE GENERATIONS. MY LIFE IS MARKED BY EXCELLENCE AND INTEGRITY. BECAUSE I'M MAKING RIGHT CHOICES AND TAKING STEPS OF FAITH, OTHERS WILL WANT TO FOLLOW ME. GOD'S ABUNDANCE IS SURROUNDING MY LIFE TODAY.

This is my declaration.

When you hear the word *legacy* you probably think of what you will leave behind or how you will be remembered when you are gone. That's one way of thinking, but there is something even more significant. The Scripture talks about how we can store up mercy for our children and future generations.

You can store up blessings and favor by living a life of excellence and integrity that will affect generations to come. I know I am blessed today because I had parents who honored God.

I also had grandparents who prayed for me and modeled a life of excellence.

You may not feel like you have a godly heritage if your parents or grandparents didn't give God the time of day. But you may be reaping the rewards of a legacy left a hundred years ago by a great-great-grandfather or other ancestors. They prayed. They helped others. It was their faith, their life of excellence, that planted the seed, and now God is rewarding them by helping you to live a life of victory.

*Your challenge is to live
in such a way as to
cause others to win.*

Every time you are kind and re-
spectful, every time you help someone
in need, every time you come to
church, serve, and give, you are storing
up mercy. It may be for your children,
for your grandchildren, or even a hundred years from now for somebody in
your family line who will experience
God's goodness because of the life
you've lived.

Day Seven

I DECLARE THAT GOD HAS A GREAT
PLAN FOR MY LIFE. HE IS DIRECTING
MY STEPS. AND EVEN THOUGH I MAY
NOT ALWAYS UNDERSTAND HOW,
I KNOW MY SITUATION IS NOT A
SURPRISE TO GOD. HE WILL WORK
OUT EVERY DETAIL TO MY ADVAN-
TAGE. IN HIS PERFECT TIMING,
EVERYTHING WILL TURN OUT RIGHT.

This is my declaration.

The Scripture talks about how all of our days have been written in God's book. He's already recorded every part of your life from the beginning to the end. God knows every disappointment, every loss, and every challenge. The good news is your story ends in victory. Your final chapter concludes with you fulfilling your God-given destiny.

Sometimes we focus too long on trying to figure out why something didn't work out the way we wanted, maybe why a marriage didn't last, or why we weren't given a position we worked hard for. You may not understand everything you've been through. But if you'll just keep pressing forward, not letting the bitterness take root, you will come to a chapter in your future that will pull it all together, a chapter that will cause it to make sense.

You may not see it yet, but God has the right pieces to make your puzzle fit together. That puzzle may not make sense right now, but don't be discouraged—there's another piece coming that will pull it all together.

8

Day Eight

I DECLARE GOD'S DREAM FOR MY LIFE IS COMING TO PASS. IT WILL NOT BE STOPPED BY PEOPLE, DISAP-POINTMENTS, OR ADVERSITIES. GOD HAS SOLUTIONS TO EVERY PROBLEM I WILL EVER FACE ALREADY LINED UP. THE RIGHT PEOPLE AND THE RIGHT BREAKS ARE IN MY FUTURE. I WILL FULFILL MY DESTINY.

This is my declaration.

A college professor took a group of students to China for a field trip. Several days into the journey, the professor experienced incredible stomach pain. He was hurting so badly the professor asked a friend to call an ambulance. He was rushed to a local clinic.

They were way back in a small town with no big hospitals. The medical staffer in charge noticed that the professor's appendix had ruptured. Poison was spreading throughout his body, but there were no surgeons around. There was little that could be done for the professor, his friend was told.

Back at home in the States, the professor's father, who is a pastor, began to feel an incredible burden for his son during a service at his church. Finally, he stopped the service and he said to the congregation, "We must pray for my son. Something is wrong."

They dropped to their knees and prayed.

Back in China, at the clinic, it was two o'clock in the morning when one of that country's most well-known surgeons walked in—the same surgeon who travels with the U.S. president when he visits China. The clinic staff was amazed to see him.

"I'm here to take care of the American," the surgeon said.

The Chinese surgeon saved the life of the professor with an operation.

The next day the surgeon said to the recovering professor: "Who were those two men that you sent into my office yesterday?"

"I didn't send anybody to you," the professor replied. "I don't know anybody here in China. I've just been here for a couple of days."

"That's odd, because two men came in dressed in nice suits. They looked like they were government officials," the surgeon said. "And they said you were a very important person and I needed to be here in the middle of the night to operate on you."

God knows how to make it all work out. . . . He is in complete control.

Even seven thousand miles away, God had people praying. That's why you can live life in peace. He knows the end from the beginning. God knows what you will need a week from now, a month from now, even ten years from now. And the good news is He's already taking care of you.

9

Day Nine

I DECLARE UNEXPECTED BLESSINGS
ARE COMING MY WAY. I WILL MOVE
FORWARD FROM BARELY MAKING IT
TO HAVING MORE THAN ENOUGH.
GOD WILL OPEN UP SUPERNATURAL
DOORS FOR ME. HE WILL SPEAK TO
THE RIGHT PEOPLE ABOUT ME. I WILL
SEE EPHESIANS 3:20, EXCEEDINGLY,
ABUNDANTLY, ABOVE-AND-BEYOND
FAVOR AND INCREASE IN MY LIFE.

This is my declaration.

God has amazing things in your future. He has doors that will open wider than you thought possible. He can bring across your path opportunity that's greater than you can imagine. You may think you've reached your limits, or that you will never accomplish your dreams, never pay off your house, and never leave anything for your children. But you don't know what God has already spoken over you. You don't know the incredible things God has coming your way.

The Bible talks about how God

rewards faithfulness. Matthew 25:21 says that when you are faithful in the little things that God will give you greater things. When you remain faithful, I believe your payday is coming.

God rewards those who seek after Him. If you have been faithful, if you have given, and if you have served then God says: "Your payday is on its way." He is about to release a moment of favor that He already has in your future. All God has to do is speak to one person, and your whole life can change for the better.

Day Ten

I DECLARE THAT GOD WILL ACCELERATE HIS PLAN FOR MY LIFE AS I PUT MY TRUST IN HIM. I WILL ACCOMPLISH MY DREAMS FASTER THAN I THOUGHT POSSIBLE. IT WILL NOT TAKE YEARS TO OVERCOME AN OBSTACLE, TO GET OUT OF DEBT, OR TO MEET THE RIGHT PERSON. GOD IS DOING THINGS FASTER THAN BEFORE. HE WILL GIVE ME VICTORY SOONER THAN I THINK. HE HAS BLESSINGS THAT WILL THRUST ME YEARS AHEAD.

This is my declaration.

I've read some on how long it takes to make wine. In general, it can take three to five years before the first wine can be bottled. And that's just average-quality wine. The better-quality wine takes between five and seven years to make. Aging it for quality and increased value can take decades.

The best wine is often thought to be twenty or thirty years old. Yet, in His first public miracle, Jesus produced the finest-quality wine in a split second, just a moment in time for what normally would take decades to do.

So, if you've worried that you don't have enough time to accomplish your dreams and goals, you need to remember that—just as Jesus sped up the wine-making process—God can do in a split second what might otherwise take you many years.

Be encouraged; the God we serve knows how to speed up natural laws. He can take you farther more quickly than you could ever imagine.

11

Day Eleven

I declare Ephesians 3:20 over my life. God will do exceedingly, abundantly above all that I ask or think. Because I honor Him, His blessings will chase me down and overtake me. I will be in the right place at the right time. People will go out of their way to be good to me. I am surrounded by God's favor.

This is my declaration.

Irene, a friend of mine, was working at home, refinishing a piece of furniture with an electric sander. As she was working, one of the main parts broke off and it wouldn't work anymore. So she put the sander and the broken part into a Lakewood Church bag that she'd just happened to have at home. She went up to the hardware store.

This gentleman came over to help her. She showed him the broken part and asked if he had it. He looked at her in the strangest way, almost like this glaze came over his eyes and he said, "No, we don't have that part. We don't even carry that model." But he reached up on the shelf and got a brand-new, top-of-the-line sander and said, "Here, I want you to have this. It's our gift to you."

Irene had never even met the man, never seen him before. She said, "Are you sure you want to give this to me?"

He said, "Yes. I'm positive. Just go up to the counter and give them my number: 5-5-5."

So she went up to the counter almost in disbelief. She stood at the back of the line. All of the sudden the lady working the register looked over and said, "Hey, lady. Come up here. I want to check you out right now."

Irene pointed at herself and said, "Do you mean me?"

She said, "Yes, I mean you, the highly favored woman."

Irene was kind of embarrassed, but the lady insisted, so she went up there and showed her the sander and said, "This man said he wanted to give this to me. He said his number was 5-5-5."

She said, "Well, he can do whatever he wants. He's the regional manager."

Just as Irene was about to leave she said to the lady, "By the way, why did you call me up in front of all these people?"

The lady said, "I saw your Lakewood Church bag and I watch every Sunday. And I know anybody that goes to Lakewood has to be highly favored."

I believe that those who stay in faith are highly favored. You need to prepare for an exceeding, abundant, above-and-beyond life; a life where people go out of their way for no reason to be good to you; a life where you get promoted even though you weren't the most qualified; a life where you find yourself in the right place at the right time.

When you walk in God's favor, His blessings will chase you down and overtake you.

12

Day Twelve

I AM SPECIAL AND EXTRAORDINARY.
I AM NOT AVERAGE! I HAVE BEEN
CUSTOM-MADE. I AM ONE OF A KIND.
OF ALL THE THINGS GOD CREATED,
WHAT HE IS THE MOST PROUD OF IS
ME. I AM HIS MASTERPIECE, HIS
MOST PRIZED POSSESSION. I WILL
KEEP MY HEAD HELD HIGH, KNOWING
I AM A CHILD OF THE MOST HIGH
GOD, MADE IN HIS VERY IMAGE.

This is my declaration.

The key to really understanding and maintaining a true sense of value is to let your Heavenly Father be the most important person in your life. Base your sense of value on what He says about you.

When you make mistakes some may criticize and make you feel guilty, like you're all washed up. But God says, "I have mercy for every mistake. Get up and go again. Your future is brighter than your past."

Others may make you feel like you're not talented, you're not attractive, or you don't have anything special to offer. But God says, "You're amazing. You're beautiful. You're one of a kind."

If you will learn to receive your value from your Heavenly Father and listen to what He says about you, then you'll feel accepted, approved, redeemed, forgiven, confident, and secure. You will feel extremely valuable and that's exactly the way God wants you to be.

Ephesians 2:10 says, "You are God's masterpiece." Do you realize a masterpiece is not mass-produced? You didn't come off an assembly line. You're not average. You're not ordinary. You've been custom-made. You are one of a kind. God created you in His very own image. He looks past all those other things and He looks right at you and says, "There's my masterpiece. That's my son. That's my daughter. That's what brings the most joy to my heart."

13

Day Thirteen

I DECLARE THAT GOD IS BRINGING
ABOUT NEW SEASONS OF GROWTH.
I WILL NOT GET STAGNANT AND HOLD
ON TO THE OLD. I WILL BE OPEN TO
CHANGE KNOWING THAT GOD HAS
SOMETHING BETTER IN FRONT OF
ME. NEW DOORS OF OPPORTUNITY,
NEW RELATIONSHIPS, AND NEW
LEVELS OF FAVOR ARE IN
MY FUTURE.

This is my declaration.

Just as God can supernaturally open doors, sometimes He may supernaturally close doors. Nothing happens by accident. God is directing each of your steps. That means if a friend does you wrong, if you go through a setback, if you lose a loved one, you can either embrace that change and God will use it to take you higher, or you can resist it and you'll end up becoming stagnant and settling for mediocrity.

Stay open for change. Don't approach change from a negative point of view. All change is not bad. It may be negative on the surface, but remember, God would not allow it if He didn't have a purpose for it. He will use it to stretch you and to hopefully push you into a new dimension. You may be in a perfectly fine situation for years, but all of a sudden you will see a stirring taking place.

Don't approach change from a negative point of view.

It's easy to become negative or bitter: "God, why is this happening? I thought I had Your favor." But a much better approach is to just stay open and know that God is still in control. If you will embrace that change, the winds that you thought would defeat you will actually push you to your divine destiny.

Day Fourteen

I DECLARE THAT I WILL USE MY
WORDS TO BLESS PEOPLE. I WILL
SPEAK FAVOR AND VICTORY OVER MY
FAMILY, FRIENDS, AND LOVED ONES.
I WILL HELP CALL OUT THEIR SEEDS
OF GREATNESS BY TELLING THEM
"I'M PROUD OF YOU, I LOVE YOU,
YOU ARE AMAZING, YOU ARE TAL-
ENTED, YOU ARE BEAUTIFUL, YOU
WILL DO GREAT THINGS IN LIFE."

This is my declaration.

When you speak the blessing over your spouse, over your children, over your students, or anyone in your life, you are not just using nice words. Those words carry God's supernatural power. They release favor, ability, confidence, and God's goodness in extraordinary ways.

We should make it our mission to speak the blessing into as many people as we possibly can. With our words we can release favor into somebody else's life.

I heard about a small girl who

had a cleft lip. When she was in second grade, other students would not play with her because she looked different. She grew up with these incredible insecurities.

One day the school was conducting hearing tests. The teacher had each student walk slowly away from her while the teacher whispered very quietly. The students were told to repeat out loud, in front of the whole class, what the teacher was whispering. For most students, the teacher would make general statements like "The sky is blue. Today is Tuesday."

When it came time for the little girl with the cleft lip, she was nervous and afraid, but after she passed the hearing test the teacher smiled and told her, "I wish you were my little girl."

When she heard the teacher's approval and the blessing spoken over her, it did something on the inside. It gave her a new sense of confidence, a greater self-esteem. Not only that, when the other students heard how much the teacher loved this little girl, their attitudes changed. Now they all wanted to be her friend.

The blessing was spoken not by a parent but by an authority figure, and it released God's favor in her life in a greater way. When she became a young lady, the little girl often spoke of that day as a turning point in her life.

It's so simple, but it can have such a huge impact. That's why you should get in a habit of speaking the blessing every chance you get.

15

Day Fifteen

I DECLARE THAT I HAVE A SOUND
MIND FILLED WITH GOOD THOUGHTS,
NOT THOUGHTS OF DEFEAT. BY
FAITH, I AM WELL ABLE. I AM
ANOINTED. I AM EQUIPPED. I AM EM-
POWERED. MY THOUGHTS ARE
GUIDED BY GOD'S WORD EVERY DAY.
NO OBSTACLE CAN DEFEAT ME, BE-
CAUSE MY MIND IS PROGRAMMED
FOR VICTORY.

This is my declaration.

Many of God's promises are in the past tense. In Ephesians God says, "I have blessed you with every spiritual blessing." He says in Colossians, "I have made you worthy." In Psalms He says, "I have surrounded you with favor as a shield."

All of those are put in past tense like it's already happened. Now you must do your part and come into agreement with God. You may not feel blessed today. A lot of things may be coming against you with your family, with your finances, or with your health.

You must be bold and say, "God, if You say I'm blessed then I believe I'm blessed. My checkbook may not say I'm blessed. The economy doesn't say I'm blessed. The medical report doesn't say I'm blessed. But God, I know You have the ultimate authority. Since You say I'm blessed, my report is I am blessed."

God has already crowned you with favor.

If you are to activate that favor, you must get in agreement with God by declaring, "I do have favor." You cannot drag through the day thinking, *Why do I always get the short end of the stick?*

How do you tap in to what God has already done? Very simple: just act like you're blessed, talk like you're blessed, walk like you're blessed, think like you're blessed, smile like you're blessed, dress like you're blessed. Put actions behind your faith, and one day you will see it become a reality.

16

Day Sixteen

I DECLARE THAT I WILL LIVE AS A
HEALER. I AM SENSITIVE TO THE
NEEDS OF THOSE AROUND ME. I WILL
LIFT THE FALLEN, RESTORE THE
BROKEN, AND ENCOURAGE THE
DISCOURAGED. I AM FULL OF
COMPASSION AND KINDNESS.
I WON'T JUST LOOK FOR A MIRACLE;
I WILL BECOME SOMEONE'S MIRACLE
BY SHOWING GOD'S LOVE AND
MERCY EVERYWHERE I GO.

This is my declaration.

You're never more like God than when you help hurting people. One of our assignments in life is to help wipe away the tears. Are you sensitive to the needs of those around you? Your friends? Your neighbors? Your coworkers?

Many times behind the pretty smile, behind the Sunday praise, there is a person who's hurting. She's alone. His life is in turmoil. When someone is struggling, reach out. Be a healer. Be a restorer. Take time to wipe away the tears.

Your job is not to judge. Your job is not to figure out if someone deserves something, or to decide who is right or who is wrong. Your job is to lift the fallen, to restore the broken, and to heal the hurting.

Sometimes you may have to trade places with someone who is hurting. You must be willing to be inconvenienced. You may have to miss dinner in order to wipe away a tear. You may have to skip working out one night in order to encourage a struggling couple. You may have to drive across town and pick up a coworker who is addicted and take him to church with you on Sunday. If you want to live as a healer, you must be willing to change places with those who are hurting.

17

Day Seventeen

I DECLARE I WILL PUT ACTIONS BE-
HIND MY FAITH. I WILL NOT BE PAS-
SIVE OR INDIFFERENT. I WILL
DEMONSTRATE MY FAITH BY TAKING
BOLD STEPS TO MOVE TOWARD WHAT
GOD HAS PUT IN MY HEART.
MY FAITH WILL NOT BE HIDDEN; IT
WILL BE SEEN. I KNOW WHEN GOD
SEES MY FAITH HE WILL SHOW UP
AND DO AMAZING THINGS.

This is my declaration.

In the Scripture, there was a man who was paralyzed. He would lie in bed at home all day long. One day, he heard Jesus was in town teaching people. He convinced four of his friends to carry him on his bed over to the house where Jesus was speaking.

When they arrived, the place was packed and they couldn't get in. They had gone to great lengths to get there. I'm sure the four men were tired. They could have easily become discouraged and said, "Too bad. It's not going to happen."

But not the paralyzed man: he was determined.

You are closest to your victory when you face the greatest opposition.

He said to his friends, "I've got an idea. Take me up on the roof. Cut a hole in it and lower me down so I can have a front row seat there in front of Jesus."

They lowered this paralyzed man down on his bed, all curled up, and put him right in front of Jesus. The Scripture in Mark 2:5 begins, "When Jesus saw their faith . . ."

That's my question for you today. Do you have a faith that God can see? Are you doing something out of the ordinary to show God you believe in Him? It's not enough to just pray. It's not enough to just believe.

Jesus looked at the man and said, "Rise. Take up your bed and walk." Immediately, the man got up. He picked up his bed. He went home perfectly whole.

There were other people in the room who did not get well. What was the difference? This man put action behind his faith. God is looking for people who have a faith He can see. Not just a faith He can hear. Not just a faith that believes, but also a faith that is visible. A faith that is demonstrated. If you really want to get God's attention, put actions behind what you believe in.

18

Day Eighteen

I DECLARE BREAKTHROUGHS ARE
COMING IN MY LIFE, SUDDEN
BURSTS OF GOD'S GOODNESS. NOT A
TRICKLE. NOT A STREAM. BUT A
FLOOD OF GOD'S POWER. A FLOOD
OF HEALING. A FLOOD OF WISDOM. A
FLOOD OF FAVOR. I AM A BREAK-
THROUGH PERSON AND I CHOOSE TO
LIVE BREAKTHROUGH MINDED. I AM
EXPECTING GOD TO OVERWHELM ME
WITH HIS GOODNESS AND AMAZE
ME WITH HIS FAVOR.

This is my declaration.

Think about how powerful water is: three or four feet of water can pick up a huge car that weighs thousands of pounds and move it all around. I've seen, on the news, big floods floating whole houses down the river. Nothing can stop the force of that water. Anything in the way is moved out of its path.

Your opponents may look powerful. They may be bigger, stronger, better equipped, and better financed. But they don't have a chance when God opens up the floodgates of His favor. You need to be ready, not for a trickle, not for a stream, not for a river. No, get ready for a flood of God's favor, a tidal wave of God's goodness, a tsunami of His increase.

You may be thinking "trickle" when God has an entire ocean to work with. You're thinking "stream" when God has a tidal wave. You should enlarge your vision. Dare to stretch your faith. God wants to release His favor like a flood. He wants to overwhelm you with His goodness.

Day Nineteen

I DECLARE THERE IS AN ANOINTING
OF EASE ON MY LIFE. GOD IS GOING
BEFORE ME MAKING CROOKED
PLACES STRAIGHT. HIS YOKE IS EASY
AND HIS BURDEN IS LIGHT. I WILL
NOT CONTINUALLY STRUGGLE. WHAT
USED TO BE DIFFICULT WILL NOT BE
DIFFICULT ANYMORE. GOD'S FAVOR
AND BLESSING ON MY LIFE IS
LIGHTENING THE LOAD AND TAKING
THE PRESSURE OFF.

This is my declaration.

Jesus said, "My yoke is easy and my burden is light." God wants to make your life easier. He wants to help you when you're driving in traffic, shopping at the grocery store, raising your children, and dealing with that problem at work. Every day you should thank Him for His anointing of ease.

I was once in a difficult situation I didn't know how to resolve. I was in another city far away from home. I really needed some advice, so I called a friend. He said, "Joel, you really need to talk to one of my associates. He's an expert in this field. He'll be able to help you. But he's out of town for two weeks."

Well, I didn't have two weeks. That was like a lifetime to me. He asked me where I was and I told him. He said, "You've got to be kidding. That man just left two or three hours ago and that's exactly where he's heading."

Here we were; both of us thousands of miles from home. We could have been anywhere in the world. What were the chances that we'd end up less than five minutes from each other?

God is directing every one of your steps.

He has already lined up solutions to your problems. He has lined up the breaks you need. I want you to go out each day knowing there is favor in your future. There is restoration in your future. There is healing in your future. There are good breaks just ahead of you. If you stay in faith you will see favor that will make your life easier.

Day Twenty

I DECLARE THAT I AM CALM AND
PEACEFUL. I WILL NOT LET PEOPLE
OR CIRCUMSTANCES UPSET ME. I
WILL RISE ABOVE EVERY DIFFICULTY,
KNOWING THAT GOD HAS GIVEN ME
THE POWER TO REMAIN CALM.
I CHOOSE TO LIVE MY LIFE HAPPY,
BLOOM WHERE I AM PLANTED, AND
LET GOD FIGHT MY BATTLES.

This is my declaration.

When you allow what someone says or does to upset you, you're allowing them to control you. When you say, "You make me so mad," what you're really doing is admitting that you're giving away your power. As long as that person knows they can push this button and you'll respond this way, you are giving them exactly what they want.

People have a right to say what they want, to do what they want, as long as it's legal. But we have a right to not get offended. We have a right to overlook it. But when we get upset and go around angry, we change. What's happening is we're putting too much importance on what they think about us. What they say about you does not define who you are. Their opinion of you does not determine your self-worth. Let that bounce off of you like water off of a duck's back. They have every right to have their opinion, and you have every right to ignore it.

21

Day Twenty-One

I DECLARE GOD'S SUPERNATURAL FAVOR OVER MY LIFE. WHAT I COULD NOT MAKE HAPPEN ON MY OWN, GOD WILL MAKE HAPPEN FOR ME. SUPERNATURAL OPPORTUNITIES, HEALING, RESTORATION, AND BREAKTHROUGHS ARE COMING MY WAY. I AM GETTING STRONGER, HEALTHIER, AND WISER. I WILL DISCOVER TALENT THAT I DIDN'T KNOW I HAD AND I WILL ACCOMPLISH MY GOD-GIVEN DREAM.

This is my declaration.

In the Bible, God promised Sarah she would have a child. At first she didn't believe it. She thought she was too old. I love what God said to her in Genesis 18:14: "Sarah, is there anything too hard for the Lord?"

God says that to each one of us. "Is there anything too hard for Me?" Do you think your dreams are too big for God to bring to pass? Do you think your relationship is too far gone for God to restore? Do you think you just have to live with that sickness the rest of your life?

No, get a new vision today. Put

on a new attitude. God is saying, "I am all-powerful. I can turn any situation around."

It doesn't matter what it looks like in the natural world. He is a supernatural God.

God is the one who puts the dream in your heart. . . . He wants to amaze you with His goodness.

When you believe, it sets a series of events into motion. God wants to give you the desires of your heart. I believe even right now, because you're in faith, because you're saying, "Lord, I believe," God is arranging things in your favor. He is lining up the right people, the right opportunities. In the coming days you will see supernatural increase, explosive blessings.

Day Twenty-Two

I WILL LIVE VICTORIOUSLY. I WAS
CREATED IN THE IMAGE OF GOD. I
HAVE THE DNA OF A WINNER. I AM
WEARING A CROWN OF FAVOR.
ROYAL BLOOD FLOWS THROUGH MY
VEINS. I AM THE HEAD, NEVER THE
TAIL, ABOVE, NEVER BENEATH. I
WILL LIVE WITH PURPOSE, PASSION,
AND PRAISE, KNOWING THAT I WAS
DESTINED TO LIVE IN VICTORY.

This is my declaration.

It says in Romans 5:17, "We are to reign in life as kings." When God looks at us, He doesn't see us defeated, barely getting by, or just taking the left-over positions. Not at all. God sees you as a king. He sees you as a queen. You have His royal blood flowing through your veins. You and I are supposed to reign in life.

Do you know what that word *reign* means? It means "time in power." God said we're to reign how long? In life. That means as long as you're alive that is your time in power.

Your term is to reign every single day, to be victorious, to rise to new levels, to accomplish great things.

New seeds are taking root; strongholds that may have kept you back for years, even right now, are being broken. You need to rise up and say, "That's it. I'm not settling where I am. I know it's still my time of power. Yes, I may have taken a break for a little while but I've got an announcement. I'm coming back. I will start stepping up to who God created me to be."

23

Day Twenty-Three

I DECLARE I AM A PEOPLE BUILDER. I
WILL LOOK FOR OPPORTUNITIES TO EN-
COURAGE OTHERS TO BRING OUT THE
BEST IN THEM AND TO HELP THEM AC-
COMPLISH THEIR DREAMS.
I WILL SPEAK WORDS OF FAITH AND
VICTORY, AFFIRMING THEM, APPROVING
THEM, LETTING THEM KNOW THEY ARE
VALUED. I WILL CALL OUT THEIR SEEDS
OF GREATNESS, HELPING THEM TO RISE
HIGHER AND BECOME ALL THAT GOD
CREATED THEM TO BE.

This is my declaration.

Do you know how many people have never been told: "You are a winner"? There are most likely people in your life right now who are starving for your approval. They are craving for you to speak the blessing over their life.

Everyone needs to be valued. Everyone needs to be appreciated. Every person needs that blessing.

Let me ask you today, what kind of seeds are you planting in your child, in your spouse, in that friend, in that nephew? Are you believing in anyone? Are you taking an interest to see how you can make someone's life better? Listen to their dreams. Find out what God has put in their hearts. Let them know you're behind them. Give them your approval.

If you talk with any successful people, they'll tell you somebody believed in them. Somebody planted a seed and encouraged them when they were down.

We don't realize the power we hold. We don't always realize what it means when we tell somebody, "I believe in you. You've got what it takes. I'm behind you one hundred percent." And really, every one of us should be someone else's number one fan. We should be encouraging them, lifting them when they've fallen, celebrating when they succeed, praying when they're struggling, urging them forward. That's what it means to be a people builder.

24

Day Twenty-Four

I DECLARE I WILL SPEAK ONLY POSITIVE
WORDS OF FAITH AND VICTORY OVER
MYSELF, MY FAMILY, AND MY FUTURE. I
WILL NOT USE MY WORDS TO DESCRIBE
THE SITUATION. I WILL USE MY WORDS
TO CHANGE MY SITUATION. I WILL CALL
IN FAVOR, GOOD BREAKS, HEALING,
AND RESTORATION. I WILL NOT TALK TO
GOD ABOUT HOW BIG MY PROBLEMS
ARE. I WILL TALK TO MY PROBLEMS
ABOUT HOW BIG MY GOD IS.

This is my declaration.

We need to pay attention to the things we say. I've known people who are always talking about how tired and run-down they are. They say it so much it's become a reality. The more you talk about negative things in your life the more you call them in. So if you wake up in the morning and feel tired and lethargic, instead of complaining, you need to declare: "I'm strong. I'm full of energy. God is renewing my strength. I can do what I need to do today."

Don't talk about the way you are. Talk about the way you want to be.

Encourage yourself.
Don't speak defeat over
your life.

Be bold and dare to say, "I look
great today. I'm made in the image of
Almighty God. I am strong and talented. I'm blessed. I am creative. I will
have a productive day."

25

Day Twenty-Five

I WILL NOT JUST SURVIVE; I WILL
THRIVE! I WILL PROSPER DESPITE
EVERY DIFFICULTY THAT MAY COME
MY WAY. I KNOW EVERY SETBACK IS
A SETUP FOR A COMEBACK. I WILL
NOT GET STAGNANT, GIVE UP ON MY
DREAMS, OR SETTLE WHERE I AM. I
KNOW ONE TOUCH OF GOD'S FAVOR
CAN CHANGE EVERYTHING. I'M
READY FOR A YEAR OF BLESSINGS
AND A YEAR OF THRIVING!

This is my declaration.

Some people lock into a survival mentality instead of a thriving mentality. They watch so many troubling news reports they decide: "It's so bad. How will I ever make it?"

Just like you can be talked into surviving, I want to talk you into thriving. I realize we need to use wisdom with what God has given us. But I don't believe we're supposed to pull back to where we're not pursuing our dreams anymore so that we don't expect increase or favor. I don't think we should just be holding on, or trying to main-tain. That is a survival mentality.

God can multiply your time and help you to get more done. He can multiply your wisdom and help you to make better decisions.

A survival mentality will keep you from God's best. Shake it off and say, "God, You promised what was meant for my harm You would use to my advantage. I may have been through the fire, through the famine, through the flood, but I know it's my time for favor. It's my time to see more of Your goodness in my life."

Keep your faith out there. I want you to start expecting God to increase you in a greater way. Start expecting this to be your best year so far!

26

Day Twenty-Six

I WILL CHOOSE FAITH OVER FEAR! I
WILL MEDITATE ON WHAT IS POSITIVE
AND WHAT IS GOOD ABOUT MY SITUA-
TION. I WILL USE MY ENERGY NOT TO
WORRY BUT TO BELIEVE. FEAR HAS NO
PART IN MY LIFE. I WILL NOT DWELL ON
NEGATIVE, DISCOURAGING THOUGHTS.
MY MIND IS SET ON WHAT GOD SAYS
ABOUT ME. I KNOW HIS PLAN FOR ME
IS FOR SUCCESS, VICTORY, AND
ABUNDANCE.

This is my declaration.

Fear and faith have something in common. They both ask us to believe something will happen that we cannot see.

Fear says, "Believe the negative. That pain in your side? That's the same thing your grandmother died from. It will probably be the end of you."

Faith says, "That sickness is not permanent. It's only temporary."

What we meditate on is what takes root. If we go around all day thinking about our fears, playing them over and over again in our minds, they become a reality.

Don't use your energy to worry. Use your energy to believe.

It takes the same amount of energy to believe as it does to worry. It's just as easy to say, "God is supplying all of my needs" as it is to say, "I'll never make it."

Instead say, "God, my life is in Your hands. I know You're guiding and directing my steps and I'm not expecting defeat. I'm not expecting failure. I'm expecting to have a blessed year.

I'm expecting to go over and not un-
der."

27

Day Twenty-Seven

I DECLARE I AM EQUIPPED FOR EVERY
GOOD WORK GOD HAS PLANNED FOR
ME. I AM ANOINTED AND EMPOWERED
BY THE CREATOR OF THE UNIVERSE.
EVERY BONDAGE, EVERY LIMITATION,
IS BEING BROKEN OFF OF ME. THIS IS
MY TIME TO SHINE. I WILL RISE
HIGHER, OVERCOME EVERY OBSTACLE,
AND EXPERIENCE VICTORY LIKE
NEVER BEFORE!

This is my declaration.

God has equipped and empowered you with everything you need. You don't have to struggle and try to make things happen. It's already in you: the strength, the creativity, the ideas. God's already lined up the right people. He's already given you the breaks you need by anointing you with oil, His blessings and grace.

When you face tough times, remind yourself, "I've been anointed for this. I will not be negative. I will not lose my joy. I will stay full of praise. I know God is in control, and I believe

He can take what was meant for my harm and turn it around and use it to my advantage."

If you do that, then one day you will look back on your life and realize that you made it through difficult times through the anointing God put on you. He gave you strength when you didn't think you could go on. He gave you joy when you should have been discouraged. He opened up a door when you didn't see any way out. Now you can look back and say with me, "Where would I have been if it had not been for the goodness of God in my life?"

God can take what was meant for my harm and turn it around and use it to my advantage.

28

Day Twenty-Eight

I DECLARE THAT I WILL ASK GOD FOR
BIG THINGS IN MY LIFE. I WILL PRAY
BOLD PRAYERS AND EXPECT BIG AND
BELIEVE BIG. I WILL ASK GOD TO
BRING TO PASS THOSE HIDDEN DREAMS
THAT ARE DEEP IN MY HEART. IF CER-
TAIN PROMISES DON'T LOOK LIKE THEY
WILL HAPPEN, I WILL NOT BE INTIMI-
DATED AND GIVE UP. I WILL PRAY WITH
BOLDNESS, EXPECTING GOD TO SHOW
HIMSELF STRONG, KNOWING THAT
NOTHING IS TOO DIFFICULT FOR HIM.

This is my declaration.

A lot of times we think we're not supposed to ask for too much. After all, we don't want to be greedy. We don't want to be selfish. I have people tell me, "Joel, if God wants me to be blessed, He'll bless me. He's God."

But that's not the way it works. God expects us to ask. James 4:2 says, "You have not because you ask not." If you're not asking for God's favor, His blessings, His increase, then you're not releasing your faith.

If you learn to pray

bold prayers, it allows
God to do big things
in your life.

The Scripture says in Psalm 2:8, "Ask of Me and I will give you the nations." God is saying, "Ask Me for big things. Ask Me for those hidden dreams that I've planted in your heart. Ask Me for those unborn promises that may seem unlikely to happen in the natural."

Dare to ask God for your greatest dreams, your greatest desires.

29

Day Twenty-Nine

I DECLARE GOD IS WORKING ALL
THINGS TOGETHER FOR MY GOOD.
HE HAS A MASTER PLAN FOR MY LIFE.
THERE MAY BE THINGS I DON'T UNDER-
STAND RIGHT NOW BUT I'M NOT WOR-
RIED. I KNOW ALL THE PIECES AREN'T
HERE YET. ONE DAY IT WILL ALL COME
TOGETHER AND EVERYTHING WILL MAKE
SENSE. I WILL SEE GOD'S AMAZING
PLAN TAKING ME PLACES I NEVER
DREAMED OF.

This is my declaration.

I want you to understand that even though life is not always fair, God is fair. And He promises in Romans 8:28 that all things work together for our good.

One disappointment is not the end. Your life doesn't stop because of a single setback. The challenge you are facing is simply one piece of your puzzle. There is another piece coming that will connect it all. It will work together for your good.

If you will keep pressing forward, one day you will look back and see how it all played into a master plan that God had designed for our lives. You have to have a deep inner trust, a confidence down in your heart that says, "I know God has a great plan for my life. I know He is directing my steps. And even though I may not understand this, I know it's not a surprise to God. Somehow, someway, He will work it out to my advantage."

30

Day Thirty

I DECLARE GOD IS GOING BEFORE
ME MAKING CROOKED PLACES
STRAIGHT. HE HAS ALREADY LINED
UP THE RIGHT PEOPLE, THE RIGHT
OPPORTUNITIES AND SOLUTIONS TO
PROBLEMS I HAVEN'T HAD. NO PER-
SON, NO SICKNESS, NO DISAPPOINT-
MENT, CAN STOP HIS PLAN. WHAT HE
PROMISED WILL COME TO PASS.

This is my declaration.

It says in Deuteronomy, chapter 9, "Today you are about to face people much stronger and much more powerful." Then comes the promise: "But the Lord your God will cross over ahead of you like a devouring fire to destroy them. He will subdue them so that you can quickly conquer."

You may be facing a situation that seems impossible. It may not appear that you have a chance. But God will take care of your enemies so you can quickly conquer them.

It's not by our own strength or by our own power. It's because Almighty God, the One who holds our future His hands, is going before us, fighting our battles, making crooked straight, even causing our enemies to want to be good to us.

31

Day Thirty-One

I DECLARE EVERYTHING THAT
DOESN'T LINE UP WITH GOD'S VI-
SION FOR MY LIFE IS SUBJECT TO
CHANGE. SICKNESS, TROUBLE, LACK,
MEDIOCRITY ARE NOT PERMANENT.
THEY ARE ONLY TEMPORARY. I WILL
NOT BE MOVED BY WHAT I SEE BUT
BY WHAT I KNOW. I AM A VICTOR AND
NEVER A VICTIM. I WILL BECOME ALL
GOD HAS CREATED ME TO BE.

This is my declaration.

The things we see with our physical eyes are only temporary, but the things we see through our eyes of faith are eternal. Yet too often we allow temporary things to discourage us and cause us to give up on our dreams.

Anything that doesn't line up with the vision God placed in your heart should be seen not as permanent but as subject to change.

We all face disappointments, setbacks, unfair situations. At times you may feel like you've been thrown into a pit. But instead of being discouraged and letting that cloud your vision, just look inside yourself. You will see that pit does not match up with the vision God put in your heart. You can say: "This is not permanent. This is just another stop on the way to my divine destiny!"

CONCLUSION

One final thought I'd like to leave with you is that if you are going to live in victory, you must have mountain-moving faith. We all face mountains in life. It may be a mountain in your marriage because you don't see how you'll stay together. Maybe it's a mountain in your finances, your health, or your dreams.

A lot of times we pray about our mountains: *God, please help me. God, please make my child straighten*

up. God, please take away this fear.
And yes, it's good to pray. It's good to
ask God to help you. But when you
face a mountain, it's not enough to just
pray. It's not enough to just believe.
It's not enough to just think good
thoughts. Here's the key: you have to
speak to your mountains.

It's not a coincidence that God
chose a mountain to represent our
problems. Mountains are big. Mountains seem permanent, as if they'll be
there forever. But God says if you
speak to the mountains, you will dis-

cover they are not permanent.

When you declare not in your authority, but in the authority of the Son of the Living God, then all the forces of heaven come to attention. The mighty armies of the unseen Most High God will stand behind you. Let me tell you, no power can stand against our God. No sickness. No addiction. No fear. No legal trouble. When you speak and you do not doubt, the mountain will be removed.

Make this final declaration with me:

"I declare I walk in the blessing of almighty God. I am filled with wisdom. I make good choices. I have clear direction.

"I declare I am blessed with creativity, with good ideas, with courage, with strength, with ability.

"I declare I am blessed with good health, a good family, good friends, and a long life.

"I declare I will lend and not borrow, and I will be above and not beneath.

"I declare the negative things that

have been in my family even for generations will no longer have any effect
on me.

"I declare that from this day forward I will experience a new sense of
freedom, a new happiness, and a new
fulfillment.

"I declare I am blessed!"

If you'll use your words to declare
victory and not defeat, you'll see God
do amazing things, and I believe you'll
live the abundant, overcoming, faith-
filled life that He has in store.

This book has been bound
using handcraft methods and
Smyth-sewn to insure durability.

The text was written by Joel Osteen.

The text was abridged
by Marlo Scrimizzi.

The dust jacket and interior were
designed by Bill Jones.

Jacket photograph by
Eric Forsythe.

The text was set in
Sabon and Trajan.